ECHO
THE STORY

A BIBLE STUDY FOR CATHOLIC TEENS

saint mary's press

4214 (PO5546)

ISBN 978-1-59982-871-8

All images are from Shutterstock.com and iStock.com.

The content in the Catholic edition was reviewed and revised by the content engagement team at Saint Mary's Press. Content design and manufacturing were coordinated by the passionate team of creatives at Saint Mary's Press.

Leader Guide Development: Michael Novelli

Sketch Journal Development: Michael Novelli, Kelly Dolan

Editorial: Kit Boss, Deb Brandt, Elizabeth Dingmann, Kelly Dolan

Theological and Historical Review: Peter Enns, Amy Jacober, Tony Jones

Video: IMAGO–Mark Novelli, Chris Bowman, Kelly Dolan, Mark Demel, Margaret Hogan

Graphic Design & Illustration: IMAGO–Mark Novelli, Mark Demel

Sparkhouse Team: Kelly Arp, Aaron Christopher, Rob Dewey, Andrew DeYoung, Elizabeth Dingmann, Eileen Engebretson, Tory Herman, Debra Thorpe Hetherington, Jim Kast-Keat, Naomi Krueger, Tony Jones, Alisha Lofgren, Jared Neher, Michael Novelli, Joan O'Brien, Ivy Palmer Skrade, Timothy Paulson, Dawn Rundman, Kristofer Skrade, Bethany Stolle, Jeremy Wanek

Special Thanks: Chris Bowman, Kelly Dolan, Monica McFadden, Caleb Noffsinger, Mark Novelli, Diana Shiflett, and Andrew Unger for brainstorming and dreaming up what this resource could become.

contents

WHAT IS A SKETCH JOURNAL?

Whether you like to draw or write (or both), we've created this Sketch Journal to help you *truly express yourself.* But how?

This Sketch Journal centers on YOUR OBSERVATIONS. This is no boring fill-in-the-blanks workbook! You won't be asked to find specific answers or to be a Bible expert. The *Echo the Story* sessions center on what YOU notice and wonder about. What you share, even if it is something you think is simple, is very important to your group's learning. You'll be amazed at how you'll connect ideas and discover meaning in what your group shares.

This Sketch Journal is designed to connect with the different ways YOU LEARN. Whether you're a visual learner who loves to draw, an auditory learner who loves to hear a great story told, or an active learner who needs to get up and move around, you'll find all sorts of exercises and activities in this Sketch Journal that connect with the way you best share your thoughts and ideas.

ALWAYS BRING YOUR Sketch Journal!

You must bring your Sketch Journal EVERY TIME your group meets. During your *Echo the Story* sessions, this Sketch Journal will guide you through the process of learning and responding to the Bible stories (see the *Echo the Story* Overview for more details). If you take this home, don't forget to bring it the next time you meet!

YOU ARE CREATIVE!!

You may think that only certain kinds of people in life are creative—and that you are *not* one of them. NOT TRUE!

Research has shown that <u>every person has the ability to be creative</u>. In fact, you were born creative. Think back to when you were a kid and some of the creative things you loved to do: drawing, coloring, building sand castles, taking computers apart and putting them back together again.

Creativity is about making connections and expressing your own unique perspective. Don't worry about how your drawing looks or how eloquently your poem reads. The important thing is that you are challenging yourself—and sharing a part of who you are. Be confident in your creativity!

If you come to *Echo the Story* and this Sketch Journal with curiosity, wonder, and imagination, you'll be amazed by how your creativity is awakened—helping you to connect with God in new and deeper ways.

THIS SKETCH JOURNAL IS YOURS. INVEST YOURSELF IN IT.

EXPRESS YOURSELF THROUGH IT.

WHAT YOU CREATE AND SHARE MAKES A DIFFERENCE.

As you flip through this Sketch Journal, you'll see that each session follows a pattern. This is the process you'll experience each time you and your group gather for *Echo the Story:*

① rewind THE STORY

You'll watch a short video clip that asks a question for you to discuss with a partner. The video then recaps previous stories, animating the symbols for each story.

② prepare FOR THE STORY

You'll quickly draw your own version of the story symbol in the Sketch Journal and then your group will read a section that will prepare you for the story.

③ imagine THE STORY

You'll listen to your group leader tell the current session's story, imagining every detail like it's a movie playing in your mind.

④ capture WHAT YOU NOTICE

You'll use your Sketch Journal to capture in words or sketches what you noticed in the story.

⑤ remix THE STORY

You'll get to choose from a drawing or writing activity to creatively interact with the story.

⑥ connect TO YOUR STORY

You'll end your group time by sharing your REMIX activities and having a dialogue with your group about what you are noticing and wondering about the story.

EXPLORE MORE: Two pages at the end of each session that give you more creative ways to explore the story on your own.

SESSION 1:
creation

prepare
FOR THE STORY

SKETCH
YOUR VERSION
OF THE CREATION STORY SYMBOL
HERE

FAIRY TALES

Fables and folk tales that contain some wise teachings

INSTRUCTION MANUAL

Life principles, wisdom, and moral truths

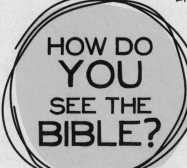

HOW DO **YOU** SEE THE **BIBLE?**

SACRED STORY

Ancient accounts of people's experiences with, and beliefs about, God

HISTORY BOOK

A literal record of events describing God's Laws for, and rescue of, humans

Like a bigger-than-life epic told around a campfire, the Bible is a sacred story, revealing to us deep truths about God and life.

Each session we will "gather around our fire," using our imaginations to enter this story and discover how it can shape our lives.

LISTEN &
IMAGINE
THE STORY
RIGHT NOW

🌍 creation 11

capture
WHAT YOU NOTICE

What stood out to you
from the story?

What did you see
or sense?

SKETCH OR
WRITE
QUICKLY HERE

DRAW A SCENE, MAKE A LIST, WRITE A PRAYER . . . ANYTHING TO CAPTURE WHAT YOU NOTICED IN THE STORY.

🜨 creation

remix
THE STORY

From the next few pages choose a REMIX activity— either drawing or creative writing— and start REMIXing!

DRAWING: STORYBOARD

Using the storyboard frames below, sketch the way you see each part of the story as you hear it retold.

SCENE 1: BEGINNINGS

1. God hovers over the formless Earth.

2. God creates the universe, including Earth.

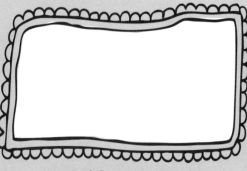

3. God forms all kinds of creatures.

4. God rests.

SCENE 2: FIRST HUMANS

1. God forms Adam from dirt.

2. God places Adam in a lush garden.

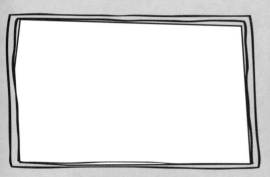

3. God forms Eve from Adam's rib.

4. God walks with humans.

This REMIX section is designed to help you retell part of the story in your own unique way.

CREATIVE WRITING:
SIX-WORD STORY

INSTRUCTIONS:

On the next page is part of the CREATION story
taken directly from the Bible.
Read these verses two times—slowly.

Then come up with your own creative way to retell
this part of the story using only six words.
This could be a sentence or six separate words.
Be creative!

GENESIS 1:26–31

Then God said: Let us make human beings in our image, after our likeness. Let them have dominion over the fish of the sea, the birds of the air, the tame animals, all the wild animals, and all the creatures that crawl on the earth.

God created mankind in his image;
> in the image of God he created them;
> male and female he created them.

God blessed them and God said to them: Be fertile and multiply; fill the earth and subdue it. Have dominion over the fish of the sea, the birds of the air, and all the living things that crawl on the earth. God also said: See, I give you every seed-bearing plant on all the earth and every tree that has seed-bearing fruit on it to be your food; and to all the wild animals, all the birds of the air, and all the living creatures that crawl on the earth, I give all the green plants for food. And so it happened. God looked at everything he had made, and found it very good. Evening came, and morning followed—the sixth day.

connect
TO YOUR STORY

RIGHT NOW:
TURN TO ONE OR TWO PEOPL
NEAR YOU AND SHARE YOUR
REMIX WITH THEM.

Jot down stuff her
that OTHERS SHAF
that connects
with you.

18

WRITE, THEN SHARE:

What do you think this story says about US?
. . . about YOU?

What does it mean for YOU
to be created in the image of God?

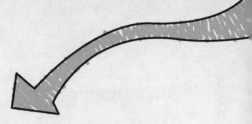

There is so much more to discover about the story!

In the next week, CHOOSE FROM ANY of the EXPLORE MORE ACTIVITIES here to help you learn more and live out the story.

SHARE

In the next 24 hours, share with one of your parents (or a grandparent, aunt, uncle, or an adult you know well) something you drew or wrote in your Sketch Journal. Tell this person why you wrote or drew what you did.

READ ✝

See *The Catholic Youth Bible* article "In The Beginning" at Genesis 1:1–2:4.

You can read a more detailed version of the CREATION story in the first two chapters of the book of Genesis (the first book in the Bible). In the next week, read Genesis , chapters 1–2, in one sitting, viewing it as two chapters of a great novel or perhaps even a long poem. See if you notice anything new or if any new questions come to mind. Add notes in your Sketch Journal as you read.

SEARCH ✝

See *The Catholic Youth Bible* article "The Beauty of Creation" at Philippians 4:8–9.

What in God's creation inspires you? a sunset? the mountains? ocean waves? Search *www.youtube.com* or *www.vimeo.com* for "nature scenes." Tons of amazing clips will pop up! Find one or two clips that look most interesting to you. Before you watch them, turn off your phone and remove any other distractions. As you watch, think back to the CREATION story and God's remarkable creativity.

This isn't homework— it's your chance to explore on your own and use these activities as a springboard to go deeper!

PRAY ✝

See *The Catholic Youth Bible* article "The Sabbath" at Genesis 2:1–3.

In the next week, write a prayer to God. This could be on the next page or anywhere you would like to create it. List everything you can think of that you're grateful to God for creating. Make your prayer as personal as possible, like you are writing to a good friend.

CONSIDER ✝

See *The Catholic Youth Bible* article "Literary Genres" at Genesis 1:1—2:4.

The CREATION story from Genesis, chapter 1, was likely written during a time when the Israelites were living in slavery and exile in Babylon. Because the Babylonians had their own peculiar creation story, the Israelites wanted to make sure that their *different* views of creation and God were passed down to future generations. Go to *Wikipedia* and search for "Enuma Elish" to read about the Babylonian creation story. Consider the similarities and differences between the Babylonia creation story and the biblical Creation account. What elements do you notice were important for the Israelites to emphasize in their story?

ACT ✝

See *The Catholic Youth Bible* article "In God's Image" at Genesis 1:26–27.

Stand in front of a large mirror. Using either sticky notes or a washable marker, write down characteristics you believe are true about God, and place them around your face on the mirror. After you've written six to eight words or phrases, stop and look at the mirror for at least 2 minutes. Think about the fact that you were created in God's image, which means that the characteristics you wrote about God are also a part of your true self.

"Most High, all-powerful, good Lord,
Yours are the praises, the glory, the honor,
and all blessing. . . .

Be praised, my Lord, through all your
creatures,
especially through my lord Brother Sun,
who brings the day, and you give light
through him. . . .

Praised be You, my Lord, through Sister Moon
and the stars, in heaven you formed them
clear and precious and beautiful."

—Saint Francis of Assisi

SESSION 2:
disruption

prepare
FOR THE STORY

SKETCH
YOUR VERSION
OF THE DISRUPTION STORY SYMBOL
HERE

A disruption is when things are thrown into chaos; interrupted and knocked off course from the way they were intended to be.

THE LENS
OF THE SOUL

"Storytelling is powerful because it has the ability to touch human beings at the most personal level. While facts are viewed from the lens of a microscope, stories are viewed from the lens of the soul.

Stories address us on every level. They speak to the mind, the body, the emotions, the spirit, and the will.

In a story a person can identify with situations he or she has never been in. The individual's imagination is unlocked to dream what was previously unimaginable."

—Mark Miller, *Experiential Storytelling*

imagine
THE STORY

LISTEN &
IMAGINE
THE STORY
RIGHT NOW

What stood out to you
from the story?

What did you see
or sense?

SKETCH OR
WRITE
QUICKLY HERE

DRAW A SCENE, MAKE A LIST, WRITE A PRAYER . . . ANYTHING TO CAPTURE WHAT YOU NOTICED IN THE STORY.

 disruption

remix

From the next few pages, choose a REMIX activity— either (drawing) or creative (writing) and start REMIXing!

DRAWING: CREATING A SCENE

Using the backgrounds on each page, create a picture of two of the scenes from today's story. See how many details you can capture in each scene.

SCENE 1: LIFE DISRUPTED

SCENE 2:
STARTING OVER

remix
THE STORY

CREATIVE WRITING:
STATUS UPDATES

INSTRUCTIONS:

As you read these verses, imagine that you are an eyewitness standing close enough that you can see and hear everything. As the scene unfolds, give status updates in the speech bubbles as you would on Facebook or Twitter, describing in your own words what is happening in the story.

GENESIS 3:1–7

Now the snake was the most cunning of all the wild animals that the LORD God had made. He asked the woman, "Did God really say, 'You shall not eat from any of the trees in the garden'?" The woman answered the snake: "We may eat of the fruit of the trees in the garden; it is only about the fruit of the tree in the middle of the garden that

God said, 'You shall not eat it or even touch it, or else you will die.'" But the snake said to the woman: "You certainly will not die! God knows well that when you eat of it your eyes will be opened and you will be like gods, who know good and evil." The woman saw that the tree was good for food and pleasing to the eyes, and the tree was desirable for gaining wisdom. So she took some of its fruit and ate it; and she also gave some to her husband, who was with her, and he ate it. Then the eyes of both of them were opened, and they knew that they were naked; so they sewed fig leaves together and made loincloths for themselves.

RIGHT NOW:
TURN TO ONE OR TWO PEOPL
NEAR YOU AND SHARE YOUR
REMIX WITH THEM.

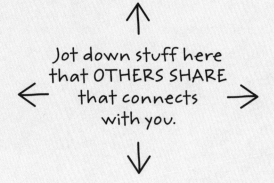

↑
Jot down stuff here
that OTHERS SHARE
← that connects →
with you.
↓

34

WRITE, THEN SHARE:

What do you think this story says about US?
. . . about YOU?

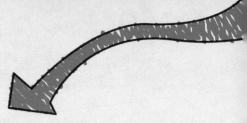

There is so much more to discover about the story!

In the next WEEK, CHOOSE FROM ANY of the EXPLORE MORE ACTIVITIES here to help you learn more and live out the story.

SHARE

In the next week, see if you can get a discussion going with one or two friends from your church group. Message them one thing that you wondered about or had questions about in the DISRUPTION story. Ask if they have any thoughts, and encourage them to share their wonderings as well. Try to keep the discussion going throughout the next week.

READ ✝

See *The Catholic Youth Bible* article "Original Sin" at Genesis 3:1–24.

You can read the entire DISRUPTION story with a lot more detail in Genesis, chapters 3 and 7. In the next week, read these two chapters out loud. See if you discover anything new by reading the story this way, and make sure to write or draw about it in your Sketch Journal.

SEARCH ✝

See *The Catholic Youth Bible* article "Sin Has Social Consequences" at Genesis 6:1–9:17.

When you think about the disruption of life, what modern-day images come to mind? Find five images—either online or in a magazine—that demonstrate where life in our world is disrupted and not as it was intended to be. Print or cut out the pictures and tape them somewhere in your Sketch Journal.

36

PRAY

Find a spot where you can be alone and quiet for 10 minutes.
Think about areas of your life or the world that feel chaotic or disrupted.
Then pray: "God, please bring peace to the disruptions in my life and in our world."

Spend 10 minutes repeating this prayer and breathing deeply, inviting God's peace into your mind and heart.

CONSIDER ✝

See *The Catholic Youth Bible* article "The Flood" at Genesis 6:1–9:17.

Many ancient civilizations told stories of a global flood. The ancient Babylonians, for instance, told a story based on an older epic called the *Gilgamesh Flood Myth*. This story is strikingly similar to the story of the flood in the Bible. One key difference is that the Babylonian story points to the existence of many (an assembly of) gods. But the Israelites' story emphasizes there being only one true God. While living in exile under Babylonian rule, the Israelites made sure to preserve in writing their own version of this flood story to pass on to future generations. Why do you think telling and preserving our sacred stories might be important?

ACT ✝

See *The Catholic Youth Bible* article "The Rainbow" at Genesis 9:8–17.

Find something in the next week that's in chaos and help bring order to it. This could be as simple as cleaning your room or the family car, or picking up trash at a neighborhood playground or park. If you need ideas, ask a parent. As you do this task, consider that you are actually helping to restore something back to the way it was intended to be.

"For when God gave great knowledge to the human being, the human being elevated himself in his soul and turned away from God. God so regarded the human being that he would perfect all his works in him. But the old deceiver tricked human beings and infected them with the crime of disobedience . . . so that they sought for more than they should have."

—Saint Hildegard of Bingen

SESSION 3:

promise

SKETCH
YOUR VERSION
OF THE PROMISE STORY SYMBOL
HERE

THE SEVENTY FACES OF TORAH

Ancient Jewish rabbis compared Sacred Scripture to a brilliant diamond. As they told the stories from Scripture, they compared it to holding up a diamond, allowing light to reflect the detail, beauty, depth, and brilliance of its many sides. They anticipated seeing something new and amazing every time they heard the stories!

*What if we thought of the Bible this way, expecting to see something remarkable and brilliant each time we encountered it—looking deeply for a reflection from this story to teach us something new?

capture
WHAT YOU NOTICE

What stood out to you
from the story?

What did you see
or sense?

SKETCH OR WRITE QUICKLY HERE

DRAW A SCENE, MAKE A LIST, WRITE A PRAYER . . . ANYTHING TO CAPTURE WHAT YOU NOTICED IN THE STORY.

From the next few pages,
choose a REMIX activity—
either drawing or creative writing—
and start REMIXing!

DRAWING: CHARACTER PORTRAITS

As you listen to the story again, quickly sketch
some portraits of the characters.
Include an object or action unique to each
character that's detailed in the story.

ABRAM

SARAI

This REMIX section is designed to
help you retell part of the story in
your own unique way.

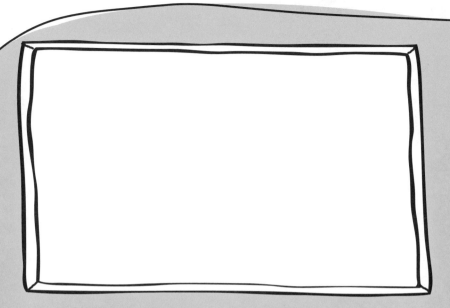

HAGAR AND ISHMAEL

ABRAHAM, SARAH, AND BABY ISAAC

CREATIVE WRITING:
IN YOUR OWN WORDS

INSTRUCTIONS:

In your own words, rewrite the section of the story from the verses below. Write it as if you were writing a short story or a part of a novel. Try to capture as much emotion and detail as possible.

GENESIS 12:1–4 AND 13:14–17

The LORD said to Abram: Go forth from your land, your relatives, and from your father's house to a land that I will show you. I will make of you a great nation, and I will bless you; I will make your name great, so that you will be a blessing. I will bless those who bless you and curse those who curse you. All the families of the earth will find blessing in you.

Abram went as the LORD directed him, and Lot went with him. Abram was seventy-five years old when he left Haran. (12:1–4)

After Lot had parted from him, the LORD said to Abram: Look about you, and from where you are, gaze to the north and south, east and west; all the land that you see I will give to you and your descendants forever. I will make your descendants like the dust of the earth; if anyone could count the dust of the earth, your descendants too might be counted. Get up and walk through the land, across its length and breadth, for I give it to you. (13:14–17)

connect

TO YOUR STORY

RIGHT NOW:

TURN TO ONE OR TWO PEOPLE NEAR YOU AND SHARE YOUR REMIX WITH THEM.

Jot down stuff here that OTHERS SHARE that connects with you.

WRITE, THEN SHARE:

What do you think this story says about US?
. . . about YOU?

explore MORE

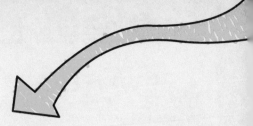

There is so much more to discover about the story!

In the next WEEK, CHOOSE FROM ANY of the EXPLORE MORE ACTIVITIES here to help you learn more and live out the story.

SHARE

In the next twenty-four hours, have a conversation with one of your parents or another adult you know well. Ask:

- *What's the greatest promise you've ever made to someone?*
- *How did you feel when you made that promise?*
- *Did making that promise change your life in some way? How?*

As you listen, consider the importance of a promise, and consider the importance of God's promise to Abraham—and how it changed his life.

READ

See *The Catholic Youth Bible* article "Abraham and Sarah" at Genesis 12:1–25:11.

You can read the entire PROMISE story with a lot more detail in Genesis, chapters 12–21. In the next week, read two chapters each day. As you read, use this Sketch Journal to write down any new details that you notice. If any new thoughts or questions come up as you read, make sure to capture those in your Sketch Journal.

SEARCH

See *The Catholic Youth Bible* article "Covenant" at Genesis 17:1–27.

In the PROMISE story, God makes a covenant with Abraham. The story calls a covenant a "deep, binding promise." But what exactly was a covenant? Search on *Wikipedia* for "biblical covenant." Read the section called "Abrahamic Covenant." Write in your Sketch Journal any details you learn about covenants and the depth of this kind of sacred promise.

PRAY

The Bible is filled with God's promises to humans. These promises can give us courage and strength for today. Take time each day in the next week to share with God your feelings and thoughts about this verse:

> Do not fear: I am with you;
> do not be anxious: I am your God.
> I will strengthen you, I will help you,
> I will uphold you with my victorious right hand.
>
> (Isaiah 41:10)

CONSIDER

The Old Testament was originally written in Hebrew. The Hebrew word for "bless" is *barak*. The primary meaning of this word is "to give something of value." *Barak* is also rooted in the Hebrew word for "knee," a reminder that serving and giving are to be done with humility and gratitude. The idea of blessing is also tied to the idea of *shalom*—a word that means wholeness, value, and to make complete. To bless is to bring shalom. Think about the people in your life that bring shalom. Make sure you express your thanks to them in the next week.

ACT

Think about someone in your life who you have difficulty connecting with or serving. Think of one specific step you can take in the next week to be God's blessing in his or her life. Be confident in taking this step, knowing that you've been created to be God's blessing to the world.

▷ Person I will bless this week: _____

▷ How I will bless him or her: _____

"Do not look forward to what might happen tomorrow. The same everlasting Father who cares for you today will take care of you tomorrow and every day. Either He will shield you from suffering or he will give you unfailing strength to bear it. Be at peace then and put aside all anxious thoughts and imaginations."

—Saint Francis de Sales

SESSION 4:
exodus

SKETCH
YOUR VERSION
OF THE EXODUS STORY SYMBOL
HERE

PARTICIPATING IN THE STORY

As the Israelites retold their sacred stories,
they invited one another to zak-hor.
It's a Hebrew word that means "to remember."
To zak-hor means more than just recounting events;
it's a calling to relive and (participate) in them.
When the Israelites listened to the stories
of their faith, they put themselves in the story
alongside their ancestors.

✴ How might you participate in these Bible stories
as you listen to them?

What stood out to you
from the story?

What did you see
or sense?

SKETCH OR
WRITE
QUICKLY HERE

remix
THE STORY

From the next few page choose a REMIX activity either (drawing) or creative (writing) and start REMIXing!

DRAWING: STORY TIME LINE

In the space below, you'll find a time line of this session's story. Near each event, <u>draw a quick picture</u> that you think best represents that part of the story.

Moses grows u in palac

Israelites are made slaves

Israel grows in number

Woman places baby in basket

Pharaoh is worried

Israelites move to Egypt

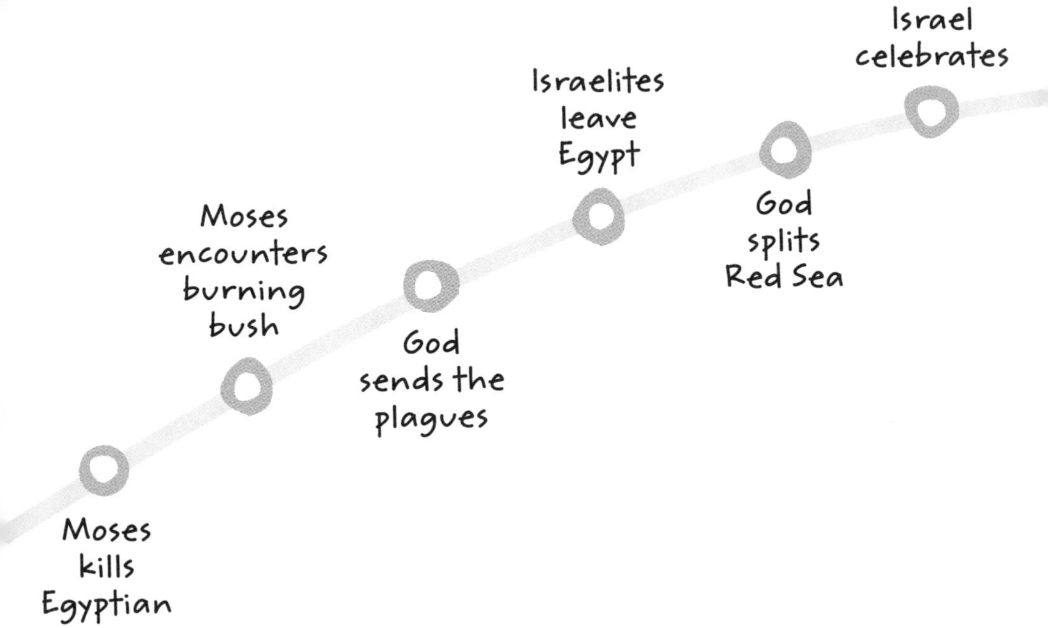

Israel
celebrates

Israelites
leave
Egypt

Moses
encounters
burning
bush

God
splits
Red Sea

God
sends the
plagues

Moses
kills
Egyptian

This REMIX section is designed to help you retell part of the story in your own unique way.

CREATIVE WRITING:
A LETTER FROM MOSES

INSTRUCTIONS:

Imagine that you are Moses and you just saw the burning bush and heard God's voice. You want to send your brother, Aaron, a letter to tell him what happened and what God asked you (and him) to do.

Use the space on the following page to write the letter you would have written if you were Moses.

EXODUS 3:4–8,10; 4:10–15

God called out to him from the bush: Moses! Moses! He answered, "Here I am." God said: Do not come near! Remove your sandals from your feet, for the place where you stand is holy ground. I am the God of your father, he continued, the God of Abraham, the God of Isaac, and the God of Jacob. Moses hid his face, for he was afraid to look at God.

But the LORD said: I have witnessed the affliction of my people in Egypt and have heard their cry against their taskmasters, so I know well what they are suffering. Therefore I have come down to rescue them from the power of the Egyptians. . . . Now, go! I am sending you to Pharaoh to bring my people, the Israelites, out of Egypt. (3:4–8,10)

Moses, however, said to the LORD, "If you please, my Lord, I have never been eloquent, neither in the past nor now that you have spoken to your servant; but I am slow of speech and tongue." The LORD said to him: Who gives one person speech? Who makes another mute or deaf, seeing or blind? Is it not I, the LORD? Now go, I will assist you in speaking and teach you what you are to say. But he said, "If you please, my Lord, send someone else!" Then the LORD became angry with Moses and said: I know there is your brother, Aaron the Levite, who is a good speaker; even now he is on his way to meet you. When he sees you, he will truly be glad. You will speak to him and put the words in his mouth. I will assist both you and him in speaking and teach you both what you are to do. (4:10–15)

connect
TO YOUR STORY

RIGHT NOW:
RAPID-SHARE YOUR REMIX IN 20 SECONDS OR LESS!

Jot down stuff here that OTHERS SHARE that connects with you.

WRITE, THEN SHARE:

What do you think this story says about US?
. . . about YOU?

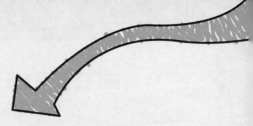

There is so much more to discover about the story!

In the next WEEK, CHOOSE FROM ANY of the EXPLORE MORE ACTIVITIES here to help you learn more and live out the story.

SHARE ✝

See *The Catholic Youth Bible* article "Holy Ground" at Exodus 3:1–6.

Go back to the REMIX activity, "A Letter from Moses." If you didn't already do the writing activity, do it now. When you are finished, take a photo of your letter with your cell phone. Choose two or three friends from your group and send the photo to them. Ask them what thoughts are sparked by your letter, and invite them to share their letters with you.

READ ✝

See *The Catholic Youth Bible* article "Moses" at Exodus, chapter 15.

You can read the entire EXODUS story with a lot more detail in Exodus, chapters 1–15. In the next week, do something a little different: read the entire fifteen chapters in one sitting. It will probably take you an hour or two, but you'll catch all sorts of new details by reading it this way. If any new thoughts or questions come up as you read, make sure to capture those in your Sketch Journal.

SEARCH

The two most famous movies that have been made about this story are *The Ten Commandments* (1956, 231 minutes, rated A-I and G) and *The Prince of Egypt* (1998, 98 minutes, rated A-II and PG). In the next week, watch one or both movies and pay attention to the similarities and differences from the account of the story you heard in this session. Why do you think the Hollywood versions differ from the biblical version? What details do you like that the Hollywood versions included?

PRAY

See *The Catholic Youth Bible* article "God the Father" at Exodus 3:13–15.

Consider writing this verse on a piece of paper and hanging it above the door to your room:

> But the LORD said: I have witnessed the affliction of my people in Egypt and have heard their cry against their taskmasters, so I know well what they are suffering. (Exodus 3:7)

Each time you enter your room and see this verse, be reminded of how God heard the Israelites cry. Talk to God about areas where you feel hurt, rejected, or alone. Take comfort that God is with you in your pain.

CONSIDER

See *The Catholic Youth Bible* article "The Passover" at Exodus 12:14–28.

For more than four thousand years, Jewish people have remembered the Exodus story through a Passover celebration, centering on a special meal called a Seder. At a Seder, each item of food and drink symbolizes some aspect of God rescuing the Israelites, and leading them out of slavery in Egypt. Symbolically, the meal itself tells the story. Consider why this story is so important to Jewish people that they continue to celebrate it each year.

ACT

See *The Catholic Youth Bible* article "God Liberates Us from Oppression" at Exodus 14:1–31.

Take a walk around your neighborhood or a nearby park. As you walk, think about what it must have been like for the Israelites to leave Egypt. Think about the journey the Israelites were embarking on, and the hopes and dreams they had for returning to the homeland that God had promised to them.

"Man's salvation and perfection consists in doing the will of God, which he must have in view in all things, and at every moment of his life."

—Saint Peter Claver

SESSION 5:

commands

SKETCH
YOUR VERSION
OF THE COMMANDS STORY SYMBOL
HERE

IMAGINATION

"For me, reason is the natural organ of truth;
but imagination is the <u>organ of meaning</u>."
– C. S. Lewis

We might think that imagination
is just something to help us escape
reality, but the C. S. Lewis quote above
suggests it's much more.

✳ What do you think it means that
"imagination is the organ
of meaning"?
✳ How might your imagination
draw you into deeper understanding
of our Bible stories?

commands

imagine
THE STORY

LISTEN &
IMAGINE
THE STORY
RIGHT NOW

commands

What stood out to you
from the story?

What did you see
or sense?

SKETCH OR
WRITE
QUICKLY HERE

From the next few pages, choose a REMIX activity— either drawing or creative writing and start REMIXing!

DRAWING: DESIGN AN APP

God's commands were reminders to the Israelites of the best way for them to live.

This might sound crazy, but try to imagine what it would've been like if the Israelites had smartphones!

On their phones, they would have had a special app that not only listed the commands, but also helped remind them of the commands at specific times when they needed a reminder.

On the following page, design a smartphone app that would help the Israelites live God's way.

Make sure that your app does the following:

  √ Displays the commands given to Moses.

  √ Reminds people of specific commands at specific times.
     (You decide when and how!)

  √ Sends notifications that help people continually keep
     God's commands in mind.

  √ Ties in with other apps on the phone to perform specific
     functions. (Like taking photos. You decide which ones
     and how!)

This REMIX section is designed to help you retell part of the story in your own unique way.

 commands

CREATIVE WRITING:
THE TEN COMMANDMENTS

INSTRUCTIONS:

The Ten Commandments are one of the most well-known parts of the Bible. Many people could name at least three or four of the Commandments.

But what do the Commandments really mean, and why did God give those specific commands?

As you read the following verses, rewrite each commandment in your own words on the following page.

As you write, try to answer the following questions:

1. What does this command really mean? Is it straightforward, or does it have any deeper meaning?

2. Why this command? Why would this have been important to the Israelites at the time the commands were given?

EXODUS 20:1–3,7–10,12–16,17B,17A,17C

Then God spoke all these words:

I am the LORD your God, who brought you out of the land of Egypt, out of the house of slavery. You shall not have other gods beside me. . . .

You shall not invoke the name of the LORD, your God, in vain. For the LORD will not leave unpunished anyone who invokes his name in vain.

Remember the sabbath day—keep it holy. Six days you may labor and do all your work, but the seventh day is a sabbath of the LORD your God. You shall not do any work. . . .

Honor your father and your mother, that you may have a long life in the land the Lᴏʀᴅ your God is giving you.

You shall not kill.

You shall not commit adultery.

You shall not steal.

You shall not bear false witness against your neighbor.

You shall not covet your neighbor's wife.

You shall not covet your neighbor's house . . . his ox or donkey, or anything that belongs to your neighbor.

connect
TO YOUR STORY

RIGHT NOW:
RAPID-SHARE
YOUR REMIX IN
20 SECONDS
OR LESS!

Jot down stuff here
that OTHERS SHARE that
connects with you.

WRITE, THEN SHARE:

What do you think this story says about US?
. . . about YOU?

 **explore** MORE

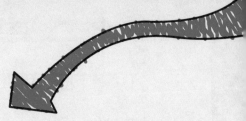

There is so much more to discover about the story!

In the next WEEK, CHOOSE FROM ANY of the EXPLORE MORE ACTIVITIES here to help you learn more and live out the story.

SHARE

In the next week, post something (on Twitter, Facebook or another social media site) that has encouraged you to live in God's ways. This may be a Bible verse, a quote, or your own thoughts. What you share might help others live in God's ways too.

READ ✝

See *The Catholic Youth Bible* article "The Ten Commandments" at Exodus 20:1–17.

You can read the entire COMMANDS story with a lot more detail in Exodus 20:1–17. In the next week, spend 5-10 minutes each day reading these verses. Each day after you read, write down one sentence in your Sketch Journal that answers this question: *How did these commands help create a better way of life for the Israelites?* See how your answers might change from day to day.

SEARCH

Go to *the Legal Zoom website and search for the article "Top Craziest Laws Still on the Books."* This article is about laws that are still in effect in some states but are extremely outdated or just plain weird. As you read the article, consider why some of these laws may have made sense at one time, and why they now seem outdated.

PRAY

In the next week, reflect on an area of your life that you feel you are not fully living God's way. Pray a short prayer to God confessing this area, and also asking for God's help to live the best possible way—God's way—in all areas of your life.

CONSIDER

When Moses met with God on the mountain, God also gave the Israelites laws in addition to the commands. Some of the laws detailed what kind of food the Israelites should and shouldn't eat. This is where the idea of eating *kosher* came from. Read more about the idea of kosher on Wikipedia. As you read, consider why—in the time and place these commands were originally given—God would have given such specific dietary restrictions to the Israelites.

ACT ✝

See *The Catholic Youth Bible* article "Living the Ten Commandments" at Exodus 20:2–17.

The commands given to the Israelites were intended to help them have the best possible relationship with God and one another. In the next week, connect with members of your group and begin creating a list of rules and guidelines that would make your group a safe and fun place for every person to grow. Be sure to share these with your group leader!

"It is not hard to obey when we love the one whom we obey."

—Saint Ignatius of Loyola

SESSION 6:

judges & Kings

prepare
FOR THE STORY

SKETCH
YOUR VERSION
OF THE JUDGES & KINGS
STORY SYMBOL **HERE**

IMPLICATED
BY THE STORY

Stories have a different way of speaking to our lives. Instead of us having to search for meaning, often the meaning of a story finds us. This is called *implication.*

To implicate means to wrap up in something, to twist together like strands in a rope.

✳ How has the Bible's story implicated you?

✳ In what ways have you begun to see yourself in this story?

capture
WHAT YOU NOTICE

What stood out to you
from the story?

What did you see
or sense?

SKETCH OR
WRITE
QUICKLY HERE

DRAW A SCENE, MAKE A LIST, WRITE A PRAYER . . . ANYTHING TO CAPTURE WHAT YOU NOTICED IN THE STORY.

 judges & Kings

remix
THE STORY

From the next few pages, choose a REMIX activity— either drawing or creative writing and start REMIXing!

This REMIX section is designed to help you retell part of the story in your own unique way.

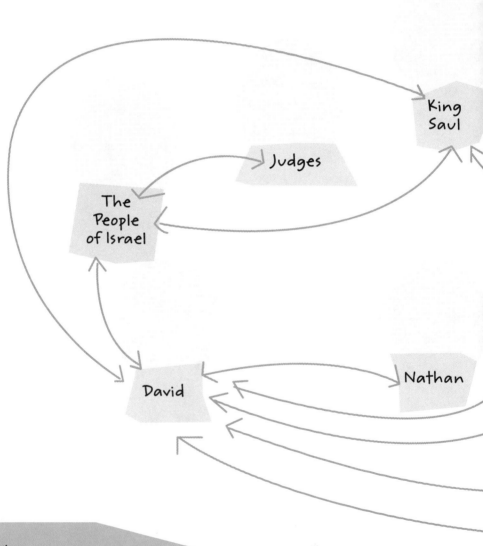

King Saul

Judges

The People of Israel

David

Nathan

DRAWING: CHARACTER MAP

There are quite a few characters mentioned in this story. Sometimes it's helpful to map out all of the characters and their relationships to one another.

1. Draw a quick sketch of each character listed.

2. On the connecting lines, write or draw how the characters interact in the story.

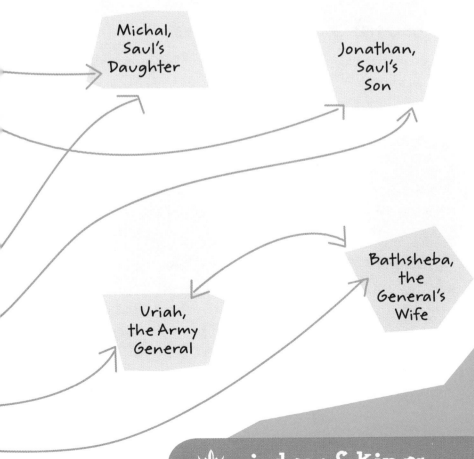

Michal,
Saul's
Daughter

Jonathan,
Saul's
Son

Bathsheba,
the
General's
Wife

Uriah,
the Army
General

CREATIVE WRITING:
SPOKEN WORD / POEM

INSTRUCTIONS:

Read the section of the story presented below and then write a short spoken word piece or a poem that tells the story of the JUDGES & KINGS. Fill your writing with action-filled, descriptive terms. This is your chance to be creative!

2 SAMUEL 11:2–5,14–17,26;12:7,9,13

One evening David rose from his bed and strolled about on the roof of the king's house. From the roof he saw a woman bathing; she was very beautiful. David sent people to inquire about the woman and was told, "She is Bathsheba, daughter of Eliam, and wife of Uriah the Hittite, Joab's armor-bearer." Then David sent messengers and took her. When she came to him, he took her to bed, at a time when she was just purified after her period; and she returned to her house. But the woman had become pregnant; she sent a message to inform David, "I am pregnant." (11:2–5)

The next morning David wrote a letter to Joab which he sent by Uriah. This is what he wrote in the letter: "Place Uriah up front, where the fighting is fierce. Then pull back and leave him to be struck down dead." So while Joab was besieging the city, he assigned Uriah to a place where he knew the defenders were strong. When the men of the city made a sortie against Joab, some officers of David's army fell, and Uriah the Hittite also died. . . . When the wife of Uriah heard that her husband had died, she mourned her lord. (11:14–17,26)

Then Nathan [the prophet] said to David . . .

"Thus says the LORD God of Israel: I anointed you king over Israel. I delivered you from the hand of Saul. . . . Why have you despised the LORD and done what is evil in his sight? You have cut down Uriah the Hittite with the sword; his wife you took as your own, and him you killed with the sword of the Ammonites."

Then David said to Nathan, "I have sinned against the LORD." Nathan answered David: "For his part, the LORD has removed your sin. You shall not die." (12:7,9,13)

RIGHT NOW:
RAPID-SHARE YOUR REMIX IN 20 SECONDS OR LESS!

Jot down stuff here that OTHERS SHARE that connects with you.

WRITE, THEN SHARE:

What do you think this story says about US?
. . . about YOU?

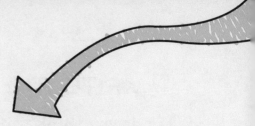

explore
MORE

There is so much more to discover about the story!

In the next WEEK, CHOOSE FROM ANY of the EXPLORE MORE ACTIVITIES here to help you learn more and live out the story.

SHARE

In this session, you only had 20 seconds to share your REMIX activity. So find a way to connect with someone from your group and share more details about what you created for the REMIX activity. You might get together with them in person, talk on the phone, or message back and forth. As you share, include key details of the story that have stuck with you.

READ

See *The Catholic Youth Bible* article "Lust and Its Consequences" at 2 Samuel 11:1–5.

In the next week, read part of the story of JUDGES & KINGS in a different translation. You can find a version of the story from *The Message* on the Bible Gateway website. Read 1 Samuel, chapters 17–18, and observe any new details or dynamics that you see in this version of the story. Note them in your Sketch Journal.

SEARCH

See *The Catholic Youth Bible* article "Wartime Women" at Judges, chapter 4.

Although most of the leaders in Israel's history were men, the Bible does contain a number of stories about women who led the Israelites. One of them was a judge named Deborah. Read more about her in Judges, chapters 4–5, and on *Wikipedia* by searching for "Deborah." What inspires you about Deborah and the way she led the Israelites?

PRAY ✝

See *The Catholic Youth Bible* article "A Fresh Start" at Psalm 51.

Some scholars believe that David wrote Psalm 51 after he was confronted by Nathan. As you read the following words from the psalm, consider if there are any areas of your life where you need to pray the same prayer.

> You will let me hear gladness and joy;
> > the bones you have crushed will rejoice.
> Turn away your face rom my sins;
> > blot out all my iniquities.
> A clean heart create for me, God;
> > renew within me a steadfast spirit.
> > > (Verses 51:10–12)

CONSIDER ✝

See *The Catholic Youth Bible* article "The Dance of Life" at 2 Samuel 6:11–19.

According to the Bible, King David wanted to move Israel's capital to Jerusalem. Jerusalem was an ideal place to rule from, because it was in the center of Israel and sat atop a high hill in the Judean Mountains. The problem was that it was controlled and fortified by the Jebusite tribe. It seemed impenetrable to David and his armies. But David devised a plan to sneak into the city through a hidden water shaft. As a result of David's cleverness, the Israelites successfully ambushed and conquered Jerusalem. This account can be found in 2 Samuel, chapter 5. To this day, Jerusalem is known as The City of David.

ACT

How might you live out what you've learned through this story in the next week? at home? at school? in your town? or even in the world? Write down one thing the story inspires you to do, and do it!

🔱 judges & kings   101

"Freedom consists not in doing what we like, but in having the right to do what we ought."

—Pope Saint John Paul II

SESSION 7:

exile

SKETCH
YOUR VERSION
OF THE EXILE
STORY SYMBOL HERE

EYEWITNESSES

Important events in our lives—a special trip,
a birthday, a sporting event—stay with us.
We never forget them.

Listening to these Bible stories each time we gather
is like being an eyewitness to an important event.
We can use our imaginations to be there—
to see the story in our minds like we're
there when it's happening.

So what you see—even if it's simple—is important to
help us each get a better picture of what this story
means to us and to understand more about God.

* What have you heard during our sharing times
that helped you to connect with God?

LISTEN &
IMAGINE
THE STORY
RIGHT NOW

What stood out to you
from the story?

What did you see
or sense?

SKETCH OR WRITE QUICKLY HERE

remix
THE STORY

From the next few pages, choose a REMIX activity— either ⟨drawing⟩ or creative ⟨writing⟩ and start REMIXing!

DRAWING: TEARING THE KINGDOM IN TWO

1. On the bottom of the next page, sketch a few key events from the story that took place BEFORE Israel was divided into two kingdoms, when Solomon was still king.

2. Halfway up the page, split the page in two, tearing towards the center of the journal so both pieces stay connected to the journal.

   > As you hear the tearing of the page, think about what it would have meant for families and friends to have been separated by this division in the kingdom.

3. Using either of the two sections, draw a few key events from the story AFTER Israel separated into northern and southern kingdoms.

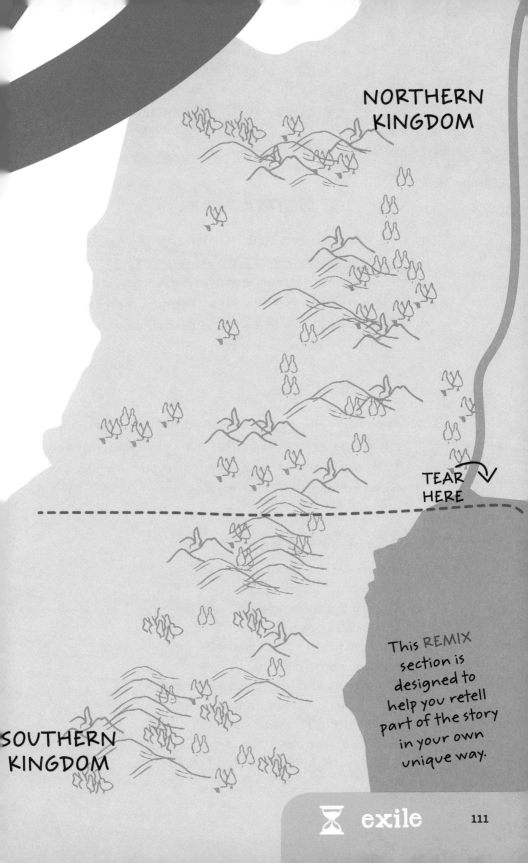

NORTHERN
KINGDOM

TEAR
HERE

SOUTHERN
KINGDOM

This REMIX
section is
designed to
help you retell
part of the story
in your own
unique way.

CREATIVE WRITING:
PSALMS OF EXILE

INSTRUCTIONS:

In the Bible there are hundreds of psalms—
<u>songs and poems written as prayers to God,</u>
often using strong, emotional language.
Many of the psalms that were written
during Israel's Exile express sadness, anger,
and cries for help.

1. Read Psalm 44 below.

2. Write your own psalm in a similar style, imagining
   you are one of the Israelites living in exile—forced
   out of your home and away from your family,
   longing for God to rescue you.

PSALM 44:2—4,10—13,24—27

O God, we have heard with our own ears;
      our ancestors have told us
The deeds you did in their days,
      with your own hand in days of old:
You rooted out nations to plant them,
      crushed peoples and expelled them.
Not with their own swords did they conquer the land,
      nor did their own arms bring victory;
It was your right hand, your own arm,
      the light of your face for you favored them.

(Verses 2-4)

But now you have rejected and disgraced us;
      you do not march out with our armies.
You make us retreat before the foe;
      those who hate us plunder us at will.
You hand us over like sheep to be slaughtered,
      scatter us among the nations.
You sell your people for nothing;
      you make no profit from their sale.
                (Verses 10–13)

Awake! Why do you sleep, O Lord?
      Rise up! Do not reject us forever!
Why do you hide your face;
      why forget our pain and misery?
For our soul has been humiliated in the dust;
      our belly is pressed to the earth.
Rise up, help us!
      Redeem us in your mercy.
                (Verses 24–27)

WRITE YOUR PSALM HERE . . .

connect
TO YOUR STORY

Jot down stuff
here that
OTHERS SHARE
that connects
with you.

RIGHT NOW:
TURN TO ONE OR TWO PEOPLE NEAR YOU AND SHARE YOUR REMIX WITH THEM.

WRITE, THEN SHARE:

What do you think this story says about US?
. . . about YOU?

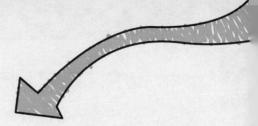

explore MORE

There is so much more to discover about the story!

In the next WEEK, CHOOSE FROM ANY of the EXPLORE MORE ACTIVITIES here to help you learn more and live out the story.

SHARE

Send a message (text, Tweet, Facebook) to someone in your group who shared something during your CONNECT time that made you think or gave you a new perspective about God. Encourage them by letting them know how thankful you are for what they shared.

READ ✝

See *The Catholic Youth Bible* article "Risky Business" at Jeremiah 39:15-18.

You can read another version of the EXILE story, told from the perspective of the prophet Jeremiah, in Jeremiah, chapter 39. As you read this chapter, notice where God continues to show love and promises to bless Israel even in the midst of their suffering.

SEARCH ✝

See *The Catholic Youth Bible* article "Holy Places" at 1 Kings 8:27-30.

During his time as king of Israel, Solomon oversaw the construction of the Temple, an immense and ornately detailed building that was a place of worship and sacrifice for the Israelites. The Bible is very specific about how the Temple was built. The detailed description of the Temple can be found in 1 Kings, chapters 6–8 , and schematics and renderings of the Temple can be found by searching for "Solomon's Temple" on *Wikipedia*.

PRAY

Pray for someone (or a group of people) you feel distant from. It might be someone you've had conflict with, or someone you just wish you were closer to. Pray that God will bless this person and will provide ways to connect you to her or him again.

CONSIDER

Many Bible scholars believe that a good portion the Old Testament was written on scrolls during the time of the Exile. These stories were told verbally over generations, but it was in Babylon that the Israelites codified many of these stories. *Codification* meant that the Israelites organized and decided which stories and details were significant to preserve. *Why do you think it was important to the Israelites to record their stories while being held captive in Babylon?*

ACT

In the next week, pick one day to fast from eating lunch or dinner. As you feel hungry, think about the longing the Israelites had to return to their home and to be reunited with their friends and relatives. (If you are not able to skip a meal, consider fasting from something else for a day—video games or social media, for example.)

"If there be a true way that leads to the Everlasting Kingdom, it is most certainly that of suffering, patiently endured."

—Saint Colette of Corbie

SESSION 8:

God-with-us

prepare
FOR THE STORY

SKETCH
YOUR VERSION
OF THE GOD-WITH-US
STORY SYMBOL HERE

SEEING THE FOREST THROUGH THE TREES

A dense forest looks very different depending on whether you are walking through it or seeing it from high above in an airplane. Both views are important. Up close, we see the detail of the trees. From above, we see how the entire forest looks.

The trees are a bit like the Bible stories we've been telling. They zoom in on one part of the great story, giving us a sense of the characters, emotions, and action.

The forest is like the entire Bible, a sweeping story that paints a remarkable landscape of God's activity in the world.

✳ What threads, themes, or storylines do you see running through the story so far?

God-with-us

capture
WHAT YOU NOTICE

What stood out to you
from the story?

What did you see
or sense?

SKETCH OR
WRITE
QUICKLY HERE

God-with-us

remix
THE STORY

↳ From the next few pages, choose a REMIX activity— either **drawing** or creative **writing**— and start REMIXing!

DRAWING: PHOTO JOURNEY

Imagine you are able go back in time and watch this story happen. The only technology you have with you is an old Polaroid instant camera.

1. Use the photo frames provided to draw the six key moments you would choose to photograph.

2. At the bottom of each photo, write a caption.

3. Next to each photo, jot down a quick thought about why you would pick this moment to photograph.

CREATIVE WRITING:
STORY HAIKU

INSTRUCTIONS:

A haiku is a short poem written in a very specific way, using only three lines of poetry:

- 5 syllables in the first line

- 7 syllables in the second line

- 5 syllables in the third line

Haikus are primarily written in descriptive terms. They include less about what is being felt, and more about what is being seen, heard, and sensed.

On the following page, write a haiku poem that best encapsulates the story, specifically these verses:

LUKE 2:6–20

While they were there, the time came for her to have her child, and she gave birth to her firstborn son. She wrapped him in swaddling clothes and laid him in a manger, because there was no room for them in the inn.

Now there were shepherds in that region living in the fields and keeping the night watch over their flock. The angel of the Lord appeared to them and the glory of the Lord shone around them, and they were struck with great fear. The angel said to them, "Do not be afraid; for behold, I proclaim to you good news of great joy that will be for all the people. For today in the city of David a savior has been born for you who is Messiah and Lord. And this will be a sign for you: you will find an infant wrapped in swaddling clothes and lying in a manger." And suddenly there was a multitude of the heavenly host with the angel, praising God and saying:

"Glory to God in the highest
and on earth peace to those on whom his favor rests."

When the angels went away from them to heaven, the shepherds said to one another, "Let us go, then, to Bethlehem to see this thing that has taken place, which the Lord has made known to us." So they went in haste and found Mary and Joseph, and the infant lying in the manger. When they saw this, they made known the message that had been told them about this child. All who heard it were amazed by what had been told them by the shepherds. And Mary kept all these things, reflecting on them in her heart. Then the shepherds returned, glorifying and praising God for all they had heard and seen, just as it had been told to them.

WRITE YOUR HAIKU HERE:

As an example, here is one of the most famous haikus of all time:

An old silent pond . . .
A frog jumps into the pond,
splash! Silence again.

— Basho (1644–1694)

RIGHT NOW:
TURN TO ONE OR TWO PEOPLE NEAR YOU AND SHARE YOUR REMIX WITH THEM.

Jot down stuff here that OTHERS SHARE that connects with you.

WRITE, THEN SHARE:

What do you think this story says about US?
. . . about YOU?

explore MORE

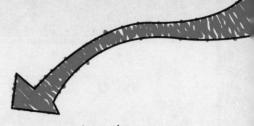

There is so much more to discover about the story!

In the next WEEK, CHOOSE FROM ANY of the EXPLORE MORE ACTIVITIES here to help you learn more and live out the story.

SHARE

In the next week, <u>share a detail you noticed in the story</u> with someone who <u>is younger than you.</u> (This could be a younger sibling or a child from your church.) Start by telling this person that you learned something interesting about the Christmas story that you'd like to share with him or her. Then ask the person about his or her favorite part of the Christmas story.

READING

See *The Catholic Youth Bible* article "Jesus' Birth: Good News to the Poor" at Luke 2:8–20.

You can read more details about the birth of Jesus in the Bible in Matthew, chapters 1–2, and Luke, chapters 1–2. As you read, keep your Sketch Journal open and capture key phrases that jump out at you from the verses you read.

SEARCH

See *The Catholic Youth Bible* article "Jesus, Emmanuel" at Matthew 1:23.

Go to the <u>*Shutterfly website*</u>. From the top menu, select "Cards & Stationery" and then "Christmas Cards." Find a card design that you feel best represents the GOD-WITH-US story. You can even go through the process of designing the card online. Instead of inserting pictures of yourself or your family, add images you find online that represent this story. You don't actually have to purchase the cards—just be creative and design one!

PRAY

See *The Catholic Youth Bible* article "Jesus' Temptations, My Temptations" at Matthew 4:1-11.

After Jesus was baptized, he began telling people: *"The kingdom of God is here! Turn from your ways and live in God's ways."*

What thoughts or actions in your life do you need to turn away from so that you can turn towards God? Spend 10 minutes thinking and praying about this right now.

CONSIDER

During the time of Jesus, Rome's emperor, Caesar Augustus, called himself the "son of god" and the "savior of the Earth." When people spoke about Caesar this way, it was called the "good news." Then, when Jesus' followers wrote about his life, they used much of the same language about him. Even Jesus used some of this language to describe himself. What do you think Jesus and his followers were trying to communicate by using some of the same titles ascribed to Caesar?

ACT

This story reminds us that God became a living, breathing human being. In the next week, find a way that you can be a living expression of God's love to someone else. Think of a neighbor, friend, or family member who has a need that you can fill.

 God-with-us

"We desire to be able to welcome Jesus at Christmas-time, not in a cold manger of our heart, but in a heart full of love and humility, in a heart so pure, so immaculate, so warm with love for one another."

—Saint Teresa of Calcutta

SESSION 9:

miracles

prepare
FOR THE STORY

SKETCH
YOUR VERSION
OF THE MIRACLES
STORY SYMBOL HERE

CREATING A MOSAIC OF INSIGHTS

For thousands of years, Jewish tradition has taught that a key way to find deep meaning in Sacred Scripture is to dialogue about it in community. They believe that the insights of many different people can help us to learn more about ourselves and God.

As we experience these stories and dialogue about them, each of your ideas and observations is like a tile—one that is uniquely yours—beautiful and creative. But when that tile is put together with everyone else's tiles, it creates a bigger piece of art—something even more impressive—A MOSAIC.

* How have you seen your ideas combine with the ideas of others in the group to form something new? What have you discovered about God as a result?

imagine

THE STORY

LISTEN &
IMAGINE
THE STORY
RIGHT NOW

capture
WHAT YOU NOTICE

What stood out to you
from the story?

What did you see
or sense?

SKETCH OR
WRITE
QUICKLY HERE

DRAW A SCENE, MAKE A LIST, WRITE A PRAYER . . . ANYTHING TO CAPTURE WHAT YOU NOTICED IN THE STORY.

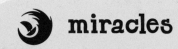 miracles

remix
THE STORY

From the next few pages, choose a REMIX activity— either drawing or creative writing— and start REMIXing!

DRAWING: MOVIE POSTER

Because this story is so full of drama and action, it brings to mind all sorts of images and scenes you might actually see in an epic Hollywood movie. So . . .

Do the following on the next page:

1. Draw a movie poster that best represents the characters and events in this story.

2. Add as many details as you can that would help people know what the story is about from seeing the poster.

3. Under the title of the film (MIRACLES), write a quick tagline that summarizes the story in a short sentence or phrase.

MIRACLES

CREATIVE WRITING: EMOTIONAL JOURNEY

INSTRUCTIONS:

1. Read the verses below, which tell the story of Jesus healing the man who was lowered through a roof by his friends.

2. As you read, write the emotions and reactions you would have had during each part of the story listed on the next page.

Think about how you would have felt if YOU were in the house where Jesus healed the man.

MARK 2:1–12

When Jesus returned to Capernaum after some days, it became known that he was at home. Many gathered together so that there was no longer room for them, not even around the door, and he preached the word to them. They came bringing to him a paralytic carried by four men. Unable to get near Jesus because of the crowd, they opened up the roof above him. After they had broken through, they let down the mat on which the paralytic was lying. When Jesus saw their faith, he said to the paralytic, "Child, your sins are forgiven." Now some of the scribes were sitting there asking themselves, "Why does this man speak that way? He is blaspheming. Who but God alone can forgive sins?" Jesus immediately knew in his mind what they were thinking to themselves, so he said, "Why are you thinking such things in your hearts? Which is easier, to say to the paralytic, 'Your sins are forgiven,' or to say, 'Rise, pick up your mat and walk'? But that you may know that the Son of Man has authority to forgive sins on earth"— he said to the paralytic, "I say to you, rise, pick up your mat, and go home." He rose, picked up his mat at once, and went away in the sight of everyone. They were all astounded and glorified God, saying, "We have never seen anything like this."

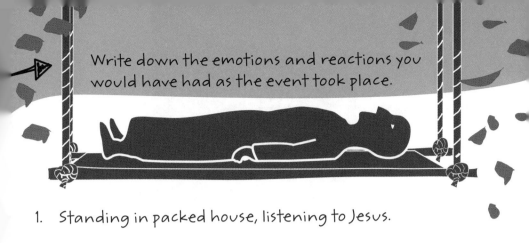

Write down the emotions and reactions you would have had as the event took place.

1. Standing in packed house, listening to Jesus.

2. Men removing part of the roof above you.

3. Men lowering their friend down through the opening of the roof.

4. Jesus telling the man, "Your sins are forgiven."

5. Religious leaders getting angry with Jesus.

6. Jesus telling man to take up his mat and walk.

7. Man standing up and walking in front of everyone.

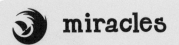

connect
TO YOUR STORY

RIGHT
NOW:
TURN TO ONE
OR TWO
PEOPLE NEAR
YOU AND
SHARE YOUR
REMIX WITH
THEM.

Jot down stuff
here that
OTHERS SHARE
that connects
with you.

WRITE, THEN SHARE:

What do you think this story says about US?
. . . about YOU?

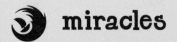

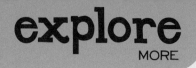

explore
MORE

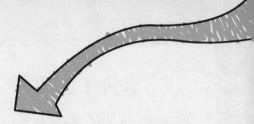

There is so much more to discover about the story!

In the next WEEK, CHOOSE FROM ANY of the EXPLORE MORE ACTIVITIES here to help you learn more and live out the story.

SHARE

Tear either the <u>Movie Poster activity</u> or the <u>Emotional Journey activity</u> from this section of your Sketch Journal and exchange it with someone else in your group. Put each other's REMIX activity in a visible place in your room or house where you'll see it often. Each time you see it, try to look for something new about what they've drawn or written.

READ ✝

See *The Catholic Youth Bible* article "Do Not Be Afraid" at Luke 5:1–11.

In the next week, read Luke , chapters 4–5 and 8–9. As you read, think about the healing and miracles Jesus performed. What amazes you about these stories? Capture your observations in your Sketch Journal.

SEARCH

There are many wondrous signs recorded in the four Gospels and the Acts of the Apostles. Find a chart listing many of these by going to *www.smp.org /resourcecenter* and searching at the top for "miracles." Find and read the document, "Wonders, Miracles, and Signs in the New Testament."

PRAY

Think of someone you know who needs healing of some kind
(physical, emotional, spiritual). Create a reminder—an alarm on
your phone, or a sticky note—that will prompt you to pray for them
at the same time each day for the next week.

CONSIDER

During the time of Jesus, a miracle or healing would have been seen as an
extraordinary event, but not something beyond belief. Most first-century
Jewish people had an expectation that God was continually active around
them. When a miracle or healing would take place, Jewish people most
often would attribute this to God's power. When have you seen something
happen that was unexplainable? Do you believe God was at work in that
event? Explain.

ACT

Who could you bring a form of healing to by encouraging them? This
may be as simple as sending a note or an e-mail, or spending time with
someone you know is hurting. Pray that your encouragement will bring
healing and wholeness to that person.

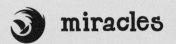 **miracles**

"Listening is much more than allowing another to talk while waiting for a chance to respond. Listening is paying full attention to others and welcoming them into our very beings. The beauty of listening is that, those who are listened to start feeling accepted, start taking their words more seriously and discovering their own true selves. Listening is a form of spiritual hospitality by which you invite strangers to become friends, to get to know their inner selves more fully, and even to dare to be silent with you."

—Henri Nouwen,
Bread for the Journey

SESSION 10:

God's Kingdom

SKETCH
YOUR VERSION
OF THE GOD'S KINGDOM
STORY SYMBOL HERE

GOD'S KINGDOM

Throughout their history, Jewish people experienced slavery and exile under the control of other kingdoms. During the time of Jesus, they faced great poverty and oppression at the hands of the Roman Empire. They longed to be free . . . and for Israel to be its own nation once again. They hoped that a new king would emerge and fight to restore their kingdom.

But Jesus gave a different vision of what God's Kingdom and its king should look like. This Kingdom would not come about through military force or domination. Jesus' life and teaching give us a picture of this different kind of Kingdom.

✳ What is one thing you thought about God that's changed as a result of listening to these Bible stories?

capture
WHAT YOU NOTICE

What stood out to you
from the story?

What did you see
or sense?

SKETCH OR
WRITE
QUICKLY HERE

DRAW A SCENE, MAKE A LIST, WRITE A PRAYER . . . ANYTHING TO CAPTURE WHAT YOU NOTICED IN THE STORY.

God's Kingdom

From the next few pages, choose a REMIX activity—either (drawing) or creative (writing)—and start REMIXing!

DRAWING: PARABLE PICTURES

Jesus often taught through short stories called parables that use word pictures from everyday life to explain what God's Kingdom is like. In Latin, the word *parable* means "parallel story."

In the space provided, draw a quick sketch of each of the items Jesus talked about in the story.

As you draw these items, consider the fact that most of the people listening to Jesus were living in poverty. How might this have changed the way they heard these parables?

A tiny seed that's planted in a field. This seed may be small at first, but it grows into a large tree where birds can rest and find a home.

A hidden treasure buried in a field— worth diligently searching for.

Yeast spread in a large ball of dough—just a little will raise a lot.

A precious pearl—worth trading everything for.

A great feast—where all of the poor and the outcasts are welcomed.

CREATIVE WRITING:
WRITE YOUR OWN PARABLE

INSTRUCTIONS:

1. Read the parables below. Notice how Jesus used word pictures as metaphors to describe what God's Kingdom is like.

2. Write your own parable. Pick a modern-day item or setting (similar to the way Jesus did in his day) and describe it in a way that would help someone better understand God's Kingdom.

This doesn't have to be long. It could be just a sentence or two. Be creative, and find something that you feel really symbolizes God's Kingdom.

MARK 4:3-9

"Hear this! A sower went out to sow. And as he sowed, some seed fell on the path, and the birds came and ate it up. Other seed fell on rocky ground where it had little soil. It sprang up at once because the soil was not deep. And when the sun rose, it was scorched and it withered for lack of roots. Some seed fell among thorns, and the thorns grew up and choked it and it produced no grain. And some seed fell on rich soil and produced fruit. It came up and grew and yielded thirty, sixty, and a hundredfold." He added, "Whoever has ears to hear ought to hear."

MATTHEW 13:44

"The kingdom of heaven is like a treasure buried in a field, which a person finds and hides again, and out of joy goes and sells all that he has and buys that field."

MATTHEW 13:45–46

"Again, the kingdom of heaven is like a merchant searching for fine pearls. When he finds a pearl of great price, he goes and sells all that he has and buys it."

WRITE YOUR OWN PARABLE HERE:

God's Kingdom is like . . .

RIGHT NOW:
RAPID-SHARE YOUR REMIX IN 20 SECONDS OR LESS.

Jot down stuff
here that
OTHERS SHARE
that connects
with you.

WRITE, THEN SHARE:

What do you think this story says about US?
. . . about YOU?

What do you think it means for YOU
to live out God's Kingdom?

 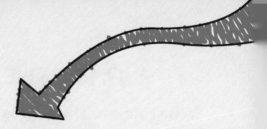

explore
MORE

There is so much more to discover about the story!

In the next WEEK, CHOOSE FROM ANY of the EXPLORE MORE ACTIVITIES here to help you learn more and live out the story.

SHARE

God's Kingdom has been described as "God's dream for this world coming true" (from author Scot McKnight). What do you think God's dream for the world is? What glimpses of that dream do you see happening in our world? Share your thoughts about this with a friend.

READ

You can read the entire Sermon on the Mount, in Matthew, chapters 3–7. As you read, think through the different people who would have likely been there listening to Jesus: his disciples, religious leaders, politicians, the sick, the broken and hurting. How do you think their perspectives on what Jesus said differed based on who they were?

SEARCH

See *The Catholic Youth Bible* article "Parables" at Matthew 13:10.

Learn more about parables and what makes a parable, by reading this PBS article. Go online and search for "FRONTLINE: From Jesus to Christ: Jesus' Many Faces: The Parables." As you read this article, think about why Jesus often chose to teach using parables.

PRAY ✝

See *The Catholic Youth Bible* article "An Upside-Down Kingdom" at Matthew 5:1–12.

Each day this week, spend 5 minutes reading through the Beatitudes in Matthew 5:3–12. As you read, pray that God would help you to grow in a way that would make your life look more like the one Jesus described.

CONSIDER ✝

See *The Catholic Youth Bible* article "Getting Personal" at Mark 2:13–17.

In this session's story, Jesus attends a dinner party thrown by a tax collector. The story mentions that tax collectors were dishonest and sometimes even criminal. In fact, they were some of the most hated people during the time of Jesus. For one thing, they were working for the Romans, the people ruling over the Jews. A frequent practice of tax collectors was to charge the Jews more tax than they actually owed to Rome, and then they would keep the extra money for themselves. *Why would Jesus spend time with tax collectors and other people who were corrupt?*

ACT

Who are the people at your school or work who are picked on or ignored? Who would your friends be surprised to see you talking to? Jesus ate with people who were considered outcasts. Pick a day this week to sit down and have lunch with one person who is considered an outcast.

"The Church is the salt of the earth, she is the light of the world. She is called to make present in society the leaven of the Kingdom of God and she does this primarily with her witness, the witness of brotherly love, of solidarity and of sharing with others."

—Pope Francis

SESSION 11:

death-to-life

prepare
FOR THE STORY

SKETCH
YOUR VERSION
OF THE DEATH-TO-LIFE
STORY SYMBOL HERE

THE POWER OF STORIES

Think about one of your favorite movies—
one that you've chosen to see over and over and over.

How many times have you seen it?
What do you like about that story?
Who is your favorite character?

Powerful stories stay with us. We can watch them over and over and get something different out of them each time. We notice different things and relate to the story in new ways.

The Bible is like this. It's a powerful story that can spark meaningful insights over and over each time we come to it.

✳ Which Bible story that we've told do you think will stay with you? Why do you think you connect with that story?

LISTEN & IMAGINE THE STORY RIGHT NOW

death-to-life

What stood out to you
from the story?

What did you see
or sense?

SKETCH OR
WRITE
QUICKLY HERE

DRAW A SCENE, MAKE A LIST, WRITE A PRAYER . . . ANYTHING TO CAPTURE WHAT YOU NOTICED IN THE STORY.

death-to-life

remix
THE STORY

From the next few pages, choose a REMIX activity— either (drawing) or creative (writing)— and start REMIXing!

DRAWING: THE PASSION

For thousands of years since Jesus' death and Resurrection, Christians have used the week before Easter to remember what is often called "the Passion" Jesus' last week before his death and Resurrection. Artists from all over the world have created works of art to represent this pivotal week.

Now it's your turn.

Pick ONE of the key events from below and create your artistic interpretation of it on the next page.

Jesus Enters Jerusalem

Jesus Celebrates Passover with His Disciples

Jesus Is Arrested

Jesus Is Hung on the Cross

Jesus Is Buried in a Tomb

CREATIVE WRITING:
PRAYERFUL READING

INSTRUCTIONS:

For this REMIX, you will spend time just reading this longer
section of the Bible, which recounts the trials, Crucifixion,
and burial of Jesus.

Read slowly, circling or underlining specific words, phrases,
or sentences that stand out to you. If you have time, read it
again. Be ready to share what stood out to you and why.

LUKE 23:20–56

Again Pilate addressed them, still wishing to release Jesus, but they continued
their shouting, "Crucify him! Crucify him!" Pilate addressed them a third time,
"What evil has this man done? I found him guilty of no capital crime. Therefore
I shall have him flogged and then release him." With loud shouts, however, they
persisted in calling for his crucifixion, and their voices prevailed. The verdict
of Pilate was that their demand should be granted. So he released the man who
had been imprisoned for rebellion and murder, for whom they asked, and he
handed Jesus over to them to deal with as they wished.

As they led him away they took hold of a certain Simon, a Cyrenian, who
was coming in from the country; and after laying the cross on him, they made
him carry it behind Jesus. A large crowd of people followed Jesus, including
many women who mourned and lamented him. Jesus turned to them and said,
"Daughters of Jerusalem, do not weep for me; weep instead for yourselves
and for your children, for indeed, the days are coming when people will say,
'Blessed are the barren, the wombs that never bore and the breasts that never
nursed.' At that time people will say to the mountains, 'Fall upon us!' and to the
hills, 'Cover us!' for if these things are done when the wood is green what will
happen when it is dry?" Now two others, both criminals, were led away with
him to be executed.

When they came to the place called the Skull, they crucified him and the criminals there, one on his right, the other on his left. [Then Jesus said, "Father, forgive them, they know not what they do."] They divided his garments by casting lots. The people stood by and watched; the rulers, meanwhile, sneered at him and said, "He saved others, let him save himself if he is the chosen one, the Messiah of God." Even the soldiers jeered at him. As they approached to offer him wine they called out, "If you are King of the Jews, save yourself." Above him there was an inscription that read, "This is the King of the Jews."

Now one of the criminals hanging there reviled Jesus, saying, "Are you not the Messiah? Save yourself and us." The other, however, rebuking him, said in reply, "Have you no fear of God, for you are subject to the same condemnation? And indeed, we have been condemned justly, for the sentence we received corresponds to our crimes, but this man has done nothing criminal." Then he said, "Jesus, remember me when you come into your kingdom." He replied to him, "Amen, I say to you, today you will be with me in Paradise."

It was now about noon and darkness came over the whole land until three in the afternoon because of an eclipse of the sun. Then the veil of the temple was torn down the middle. Jesus cried out in a loud voice, "Father, into your hands I commend my spirit"; and when he had said this he breathed his last. The centurion who witnessed what had happened glorified God and said, "This man was innocent beyond doubt." When all the people who had gathered for this spectacle saw what had happened, they returned home beating their breasts; but all his acquaintances stood at a distance, including the women who had followed him from Galilee and saw these events.

Now there was a virtuous and righteous man named Joseph who, though he was a member of the council, had not consented to their plan of action. He came from the Jewish town of Arimathea and was awaiting the kingdom of God. He went to Pilate and asked for the body of Jesus. After he had taken the body down, he wrapped it in a linen cloth and laid him in a rock-hewn tomb in which no one had yet been buried. It was the day of preparation, and the sabbath was about to begin. The women who had come from Galilee with him followed behind, and when they had seen the tomb and the way in which his body was laid in it, they returned and prepared spices and perfumed oils. Then they rested on the sabbath according to the commandment.

RIGHT NOW:

RAPID–SHARE YOUR REMIX IN 20 SECONDS OR LESS.

Jot down stuff here that OTHERS SHARE that connects with you.

WRITE, THEN SHARE:

Take a moment in quiet to write your thoughts
and feelings about Jesus' life, death,
and Resurrection.

This should be something personal for you—
a response from your heart about this story.
It could be a prayer, a journal entry,
or it could be a list of questions . . .
whatever you want to write.

explore MORE

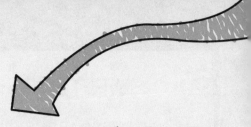

There is so much more to discover about the story!

In the next WEEK, CHOOSE FROM ANY of the EXPLORE MORE ACTIVITIES here to help you learn more and live out the story.

SHARE

This week, <u>send an e-mail to the pastor of your church.</u> Tell him one new thing you noticed in the DEATH-TO-LIFE story. Also, remember to thank him for teaching your church about Jesus and for helping you to learn to live in God's ways.

READ ✝

See *The Catholic Youth Bible* article "Jesus Strengthens Our Faith" at Mark 16:1–20.

You can read the entire story of Jesus' death and Resurrection with a lot more detail in Mark, chapters 15–16. This week, try something different. Read this story either while it is dark outside or in a dark room where you live. Light a candle, and read chapter 15 by candlelight. When you get to chapter 16, turn the lights on in the room. How does changing the atmosphere of the room affect the way you read the story?

SEARCH

No one knows the exact location where Jesus was crucified. There is a place outside Jerusalem that people visit that might provide an idea of what the location and terrain were like. It is called the <u>Cliff at the Garden Tomb</u>, featuring a rock formation that resembles a skull. (The Bible describes the location of Jesus' Crucifixion as Golgotha, meaning *Skull Hill*.)

Search for "Cliff at the Garden Tomb," and you should find images of this place

PRAY

See *The Catholic Youth Bible* article "A Prayer for Friends" at John, chapter 17.

Each day for the next week, read Jesus' prayer from John 's Gospel (below) and join with Jesus in praying for unity among those who follow him.

> "I pray not only for them, but also for those who will believe in me through their word, so that they may all be one, as you, Father, are in me and I in you, that they also may be in us, that the world may believe that you sent me." (17:20–21)

CONSIDER

In the centuries that followed Jesus' death and Resurrection, Christians created a visual way to commemorate Jesus' sacrifice, called the Stations of the Cross. Fourteen key moments of Jesus' journey to the cross are represented through art, written prayers, and readings. For more than a thousand years these stations have given people opportunities to remember, meditate, and give thanks for Jesus' sacrifice. Today, many Christian traditions use some form of the Stations of the Cross in their worship, though they are mainly associated with Catholicism. Consider learning more about the Stations of the Cross and how people continue to be inspired by them.

ACT

Our story ended today with *life*—a resurrected Jesus reunited with his disciples. How might you bring life to something or someone in the next week? This could be a relationship, an item in your house, or an area in your city. Pray that God would help you see the place where you can bring life, and then bring it!

"Let the risen Jesus enter your life, welcome him
as a friend, with trust: he is life!"

—Pope Francis

SESSION 12:

the church

SKETCH
YOUR VERSION
OF THE CHURCH
STORY SYMBOL HERE

SHAPED BY THE STORY

"Our lives as human beings are made up of stories
that have shaped, or are shaping, who we are.
The story of the Bible has the power to make sense
of all the other stories of your life. When it is
internalized and it becomes your story, it gives
meaning in the midst of meaninglessness and value
in the midst of worthlessness. Your personal story
will find grounding in creation, guidance in crises,
reformation in redemption, and direction in
its destination. People become Christians when
their own stories merge with, and are understood
in the light of, God's story."

— Preben Vang and Terry Carter, *Telling God's Story*

✱ How do you think the Bible story can
make sense of our own stories?

✱ How has the story of the Bible been changing your life?

What stood out to you
from the story?

What did you see
or sense?

SKETCH OR
WRITE
QUICKLY HERE

DRAW A SCENE, MAKE A LIST, WRITE A PRAYER . . . ANYTHING TO CAPTURE WHAT YOU NOTICED IN THE STORY.

DRAWING & CREATIVE WRITING:
REMIX THE WHOLE STORY

1. Find a partner and choose <u>one person to WRITE and one to DRAW</u>.

2. Work together with your partner to draw a sketch and write a summary for ALL twelve stories spread across the next few pages. Make sure you fill in both of your Sketch Journals. Go!

DRAW A SKETCH

DRAW A SKETCH

1. Creation

2. Disruption

WRITE A SUMMARY

WRITE A SUMMARY

DRAW A SKETCH

DRAW A SKETCH

3. Promise

4. Exodus

WRITE A SUMMARY

WRITE A SUMMARY

DRAW A SKETCH

DRAW A SKETCH

5. Commands

6. Judges & Kings

WRITE A SUMMARY

WRITE A SUMMARY

CONTINUED ON THE NEXT PAGE!

 the church

DRAW A SKETCH

8. God-with-Us

WRITE A SUMMARY

DRAW A SKETCH

7. Exile

WRITE A SUMMARY

DRAW A SKETCH

9. Miracles

WRITE A SUMMARY

DRAW A SKETCH

10. God's Kingdom

WRITE A SUMMARY

DRAW A SKETCH

11. Death-to-Life

WRITE A SUMMARY

DRAW A SKETCH

12. The Church

WRITE A SUMMARY

RIGHT NOW:

YOU AND YOUR PARTNER WILL SHARE YOUR REMIX WITH THE ENTIRE GROUP IN 30 SECONDS OR LESS.

NOW, THINK ABOUT ALL OF THE STORIES WE HAVE HEARD TOGETHER, THE ONES YOU JUST REMIXED . . .

What do you notice about God
from all of the stories?

Jot down stuff here that
OTHERS SHARE that connects with you.

WRITE, THEN SHARE:

How do you think this story
continues with us (our group)?

How are YOU are a part of this story?

explore MORE

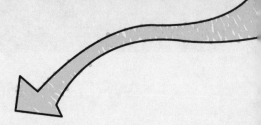

There is so much more to discover about the story!

In the next WEEK, CHOOSE FROM ANY of the EXPLORE MORE ACTIVITIES here to help you learn more and live out the story.

SHARE

Write a letter or send a message to one of your group leaders this week. Share with them how going through the story of the Bible has inspired or challenged you.

READ ✝

See *The Catholic Youth Bible* article "In Depth" in the Acts of the Apostles introduction.

The story of how THE CHURCH began is told in the Book of Acts in the Bible. It is an amazing book, depicting the remarkable adventures of Jesus' earliest followers. In the next week, read the entire Book of Acts by reading four chapters per day. As you read, note which stories most inspire or challenge you, and why.

SEARCH

Search back through this entire Sketch Journal to find the one story that stands out for you the most from the past twelve sessions. Then reread every page from that session, bringing back to mind the things you were thinking and feeling as you experienced that session's story.

PRAY

Begin to incorporate this simple, one-sentence prayer into your morning routine. Before you begin your day, pray:

> "God, remind me of your great story today, and show me how it can continue through me. . . ."

If it helps you to remember, write the verse out on a piece of paper and tape it where you'll see it every morning.

CONSIDER

Do a search for "Bible Gateway 61 Day Reading Plan." The first result should take you to a sixty-one-day reading plan that helps you to read through key Bible stories, including the stories we've heard, plus many more. Consider other symbols you would develop for the additional Bible stories you read over the next two months.

ACT

See *The Catholic Youth Bible* article "Christian Community" at Acts 2:42–47.

Go back and read what the first church was like in Acts, chapter 2. Pick one thing that the early Church did together, and ask a few friends from your group (or perhaps your whole group) to try it. This may be a meal, a serving opportunity, or working together to help someone in need.

"Christ has no body but yours, no hands, no feet on earth but yours. Yours are the eyes through which he looks with compassion on this world. Yours are the feet with which he walks to do good. Yours are the hands with which he blesses all the world. Yours are the hands, yours are the feet, yours are the eyes, you are his body. Christ has no body now but yours."

—Saint Teresa of Ávila

ACKNOWLEDGMENTS

The quotation on page 102 is from "Homily of His Holiness John Paul II, Oriole Park at Camden Yards, Baltimore" (October 8, 1995), number 7, at *http://w2.vatican.va/content/john -paul-ii/en/homilies/1995/documents/hf_jp-ii_hom_19951008_baltimore.html*. Copyright © Libreria Editrice Vaticana (LEV).

The quotation on page 166 is from "Homily of the Holy Father Francis, Saint Peter's Square" (May 18, 2013), at *http://w2.vatican.va/content/francesco/en/speeches/2013/may /documents/papa-francesco_20130518_veglia-pentecoste.html*. Copyright © LEV.

The quotation on page 182 is from "Homily of Pope Francis, Vatican Basilica" (March 30, 2013), number 2, at *http://w2.vatican.va/content/francesco/en/homilies/2013/documents/papa -francesco_20130330_veglia-pasquale.html*. Copyright © LEV.

The quote on page 185 is from *Telling God's Story: The Biblical Narrative from Beginning to End*, Preben Vang & Terry Carter (Nashville, TN: Broadman & Holman Publishers, 2006), page 9. Copyright © 2006 by Preben Vang and Terry G. Carter. All rights reserved.

To view copyright terms and conditions for Internet materials cited here, log on to the home pages for the referenced websites.

During this book's preparation, all citations, facts, figures, names, addresses, telephone numbers, Internet URLs, and other pieces of information cited within were verified for accuracy. The authors and Saint Mary's Press staff have made every attempt to reference current and valid sources, but we cannot guarantee the content of any source, and we are not responsible for any changes that may have occurred since our verification. If you find an error in, or have a question or concern about, any of the information or sources listed within, please contact Saint Mary's Press at smpress@smp.org.

sketches & notes

sketches & notes

sketches & notes

sketches & notes

sketches & notes